I'LL DO IT
DIFFERENTLY
NEXT TIME

A California Homeowner's Guide to a
Successful Home Improvement Project

Michael Jenkins

Renaissance
DOORS & WINDOWS
Fullerton, California

Publisher's Cataloging-in-Publication Data
Jenkins, Michael
      I'll do it differently next time : a California
homeowner's guide to a successful
home improvement / by Michael Jenkins. –
Fullerton, CA : Renaissance Doors & Windows,
2003.

      p.   ;   cm.

   ISBN 0-9723934-0-4
      1. Dwellings–Maintenance and repair–
Amateurs' manuals. 2. Dwellings–Remodeling—
Amateurs' manuals. I. Title.

TH4816 .J46 2003   2002094230
643.7–dc2l   0301

Project coordination by Jenkins Group, Inc. • www.bookpublishing.com
Cover design by Ann Pellegrino
Interior design by Theresa Baehr

Printed in the United States of America

06 05 04 03 02 • 5 4 3 2 1

Preface

After twenty-four years in the home improvement and remodeling business, I've managed and completed over twenty thousand projects valued at over $1 million. What I've learned over the years is that most homeowners don't know how to successfully coordinate a home improvement.

Homeowners have been very good to me. They've allowed me to have a career, they support my family, my employees, and my company, but the risks they take with their money and their homes is astonishing. I'm not just picking on homeowners that lack a formal education. I'm talking about doctors, lawyers, business owners, C.E.O.'s and presidents of huge corporations. Most don't know what they're doing either.

It used to frustrate and sadden me when I heard homeowners talking poorly about their bad experiences with contractors. I've heard so many stories about homeowners losing their deposits, not getting their projects ever completed, not getting a warranty that was promised to them, having liens placed on their property, and getting the run-around from contractors, that I was sometimes embarrassed to admit that I was a contractor, until I realized that it wasn't always the fault of the contractor, but more often it was the fault of the homeowner who had hired him.

So I decided to take my experiences, knowledge, and understanding of the industry and write this book. I figured if I could educate homeowners on how to hire contractors, how to reduce their risks, and how to eliminate the headaches associated with remodeling, homeowners would benefit and so would contractors, especially the professional contractors.

If you will take the time to read my short book, I'll show you how to avoid the pitfalls and headaches associated with bad contracting. I'll teach you what to expect and how to plan the entire process from start to finish. You'll learn how to select the right contractor, control your money, and protect yourself from liens being placed on your property.

Your home is typically one of your largest investments. Decorating and remodeling it can be, and should be, an enjoyable experience, free of headaches, lawsuits, frustration, and friction. Read on, learn from experience and knowledge, put the lessons to use, and enjoy your next home improvement.

Contents

Chapter 1

Home Improvements Are Perpetual

Being a homeowner is a wonderful experience. However, all homes eventually need repairs and upgrades as time goes on. Upgrading and beautifying your home should be a positive, uplifting experience, shouldn't it? Maybe! Psychologists say the upheaval inherent in remodeling can spread from the kitchen and bath through the very fiber of a relationship. Families fight about the color of tile, lack of privacy, clutter, mess and money. Marriages get demolished right along with the old fixtures. How you handle the coordination of the home improvements will determine if being a homeowner is still a wonderful experience.

Webster's refers to "Home Improvements" as the repairing, remodeling, altering, converting, modernizing, or adding square footage to residential property. Some examples of home improvements are the construction, erection, replacement, or improvement of doors and windows, landscaping, kitchens and baths, carpeting, driveways, roofs, swimming pools, spas and hot tubs, carpentry, moldings, woodworking, shelves and built-ins, painting, siding, drywall, plastering, stucco, chimney repair, fences, porches, garages, wine cellars, gazebos, awnings, patio covers, decks, and room additions.

Virtually everybody who has embarked on a home improvement odyssey has a horror story about lack of quality, numerous delays, nightmare contractors, and excessive over budget costs. Some delays are unavoidable, such as weather delays, acts of God, and supplier problems, but most home improvement problems are caused by the homeowner's poor planning, poor selection of contractors, acceptance of incorrect paperwork and documents, and simply not understanding the business side of hiring a contractor. In other words, they mostly have themselves to blame.

If you're a long time homeowner, you know from experience that remodeling and home improvements are perpetual. Every year brings reason to hire out a project or two or three. Let's face it, homes wear out, styles change, and kids are very hard on your surroundings, so remodeling is continuous. If you're a first time homeowner or you've owned ten different homes, pay attention, take notes, highlight different chapters, and trust this book. You don't want to be a statistic. Home improvements are a part of life as a homeowner. You can choose to understand the rules of the game and win, or muddle through one bad experience after another. The choice is yours.

> If you're a homeowner, you will eventually hire someone to work on your home
>
> For best results, understand and play by the rules

Chapter 2

What to Expect When Doing a Home Improvement

Coordinating a successful home improvement project is going to require significant time up front for planning, researching, designing, and hiring the right people. There are some shortcuts, such as hiring a contractor that has already done some work for a family member or a neighbor and comes highly recommended. But even when a contractor has been recommended to you, you still need to be cautious. There are many more steps along the way to make the home improvement go smoothly, which I'll explain in the following chapters.

Expect inconveniences. In most cases, you'll be living in the home while work is being done on it. Walls get taken down, your water or power may be shut down, bathrooms and kitchen facilities may be disconnected, and there will definitely be a loss of privacy. There will be dust and debris, and your furniture, appliances, and electronic equipment may need to be moved. Workers will be using your bathroom, toilets, and sinks. Your valuables need to be secured to avoid any temptations of theft by a laborer. Prepare yourself and your family for these inconveniences.

So start with good, blunt communication. Before any work begins, ask your contractor what inconveniences will occur, and plan for them. Also make sure all family members understand what is to occur. That way, both you and your family members, and your contractors can avoid conflicts when inconveniences do occur. For example, find out what their policy is on moving furniture, appliances, and electronic equipment. Instruct the contractors on which bathroom is to be used by the workers. Get a firm commitment on the starting and quitting time at your jobsite each day and verify that you'll have workers at your home every day until completion. Try to get an idea of how many workers will be at your home daily. Your time is valuable, so coordinate a work schedule that won't interfere with you going to your job and making a living. If you won't be there, always leave clear instructions to the workmen for access to your home.

Of course, whatever agreements you make with your contractor on these issues need to be in writing for future reference. The more upfront communication you have with your contractors, and the more details you get documented on the agreement, the better your project will go.

Expect temporary inconveniences

All agreements and details must be in writing

Communicate the smallest details with your contractor and family

Keep open lines of communication and put all agreements in writing

Chapter 3

Home Improvements Are to Be Taken Seriously

When hiring someone to do a home improvement for you, you need to take it as seriously as you would buying a new home, a new car, or getting a new mortgage. It is a business transaction, a legal and binding contract that needs to be well planned, organized, and thought out BEFORE you sign anything and make the commitment. If you are not willing to spend the time and read and understand the contract and all the documents, don't do the project. The risk of poor workmanship, poor value for your dollar, incredible stress and anxiety, and possible loss or forfeiture of money is real. Do it right or don't do it at all!

It will be crucial to have a good working relationship with your contractors, but remember you've got a business relationship, not a friendship. Play by the remodeling rules. Hold him accountable for the project and your money. Just because you might like him and trust him, don't cut him any slack. For example, get ALL change orders (see Chapter 17) in writing even though you discussed it and thought both of you were clear. You don't want to find yourself with the unpleasant shock of an inflated final bill because there are significant charges for all the changes that were made. Nor do you want the changes to be done incorrectly. Don't drink beer at the end of each working day with the guys. Wait until the job is done to your satisfaction, and then enjoy a martini or some champagne with them. Many home-owners get too friendly with their contractors, and then feel uncomfortable discussing poor quality or any other issues because they've developed a friendship.

If someone talks to you about being your own general contractor, or "Owner/Builder," they are doing you no favor. Being an "Owner/Builder" means "you," not the contractor you hire, will assume responsibility for the overall job, which may include such things as city fees, permits, fines, state and federal taxes, workers compensation, or other legal liabilities. Unless you are an expert in construction, it is best to leave these matters to your professional contractor.

A majority of complaints filed by consumers involve contractors who get in over their heads by taking on projects they don't have the ability to perform. A good door and window contractor, with an excellent reputation in his specialty, will not be qualified to remodel your kitchen or build you a room addition. As the home improvement industry has become specialized, experience is critical to quality. For best results, hire a remodeling contractor who has completed many similar projects to the one you are planning.

Always get a written contract for even the smallest jobs, and be specific about what you want done. For example, specify exact materials. If you want kitchen cabinets made of solid, red oak wood don't accept "oak cabinets" on your documents because you'll probably end up with oak veneer kitchen cabinets, which costs significantly less. If you do not specify and get it in writing you won't be getting what you want and paid for. The more specific you can detail the materials, design, and expectations, the fewer chances you'll have of miscommunications, heartache, headaches, and hassles with your contractor.

Most licensed contractors are competent, honest, hardworking, and financially responsible. However, all contractors are in business to make money for them, their business, and their employees, so be careful. A responsible and informed consumer knows that the "buyer beware" principle can help prevent, or minimize, frustration and disappointment. By carefully considering what you want to have done on your property, knowing what it will realistically cost to do the job, and what kind of professional should be brought in to do the job, you may avoid many of the headaches associated with remodeling.

Be sure to read all the documents thoroughly before you sign anything

View your contractor as a business partner, not a friend

Verify the contractor is qualified for your job

Avoid miscommunications and get your best value by being specific

Chapter 4

Planning a Home Improvement

Poor planning can be a major cause of disappointment when undertaking a home improvement project. So plan this out just like you'd plan a wedding, a vacation, a term paper, or a business transaction of another kind. If this is your first time doing a home improvement, go extra slowly and understand the remodeling rules.

What do you want the finished project to look like? In today's world, it's pretty easy to get some visual design ideas. You can look through home improvement magazines, visit some newly built model homes, or look on the internet for some ideas. You might also visit some neighbors who might have completed a similar project, visit a local home improvement store, or spend a couple of hours walking a home and garden show. You're sure to get some ideas of what is possible, and probably find something close to what you're looking to do. Collect brochures, cut out pictures from magazines, download pictures from the Internet, but somehow gather ideas of what you want to have done. All your background work will make it easier to describe (to the potential contractors) what you want.

Generally, collecting bids from three or more contractors will take two to six weeks. Once you've hired the right contractor, you still might need to wait another four to twelve weeks to start the project. Once the project gets started, the work may take from just a few days to as much as two to four months. If you've decided to hire an architect or interior designer to assist you with designs, plans, and specifications, you may need to add one to four months to your schedule. How does this fit into your life and your plans? Will the timing interfere with a vacation, relatives in town, or the holidays? Think it through. Work around a schedule that fits you and your life.

Although you might not have any idea how much the project may cost until you get some bids, decide on a budget. You may have no idea what all this will cost, but how much can you afford today? Have you thought about getting some financing? If so, add two to four weeks to your planning process.

Are you doing just a single home improvement, or will there be multiple contractors used for multiple projects? Try to plan out which parts of the house you'd prefer to work on first. And remember, if you're doing multiple projects with multiple contractors, start at the top of the house and work your way down. For example, if you're getting new doors and windows installed, don't install brand new carpet or a hardwood flooring prior to the doors and windows being installed. It would be a risk to have the workers walking all over your new flooring.

If your home improvement is on the exterior of your home, you should consult with your homeowners association prior to discussing anything with contractors. Find out if your remodeling ideas will be acceptable to the association and what requirements they will have if you decide to go forward with the project. Generally they will want an application submitted with drawings of the proposed work and approvals from all your neighbors prior to the work being done. Some building departments may require an approval from your homeowners association before they'll issue a building permit. Following this step early in the planning process may save you many hours and many dollars.

Since thoughtful, carefully prepared, detailed plans will be helpful in getting accurate bids from contractors, you may want to seek out some advice from an architect, draftsman, or an interior designer. This will make the bidding process more of an exact science because all the contractors will be bidding off the same plans.

Develop a set of plans with as many visuals as possible

Consult with professionals while developing your plans

Use a calendar to develop a time chart of the entire process

You should have a budget in mind before you ask for bids

For multiple home improvements, schedule the work starting at the top of the house and work your way down

Chapter 5

When to Remodel

D on't remodel or hire a home improvement contractor when every other homeowner in America is doing a home improvement. When contractors are busy, prices are high and response time is slower. Try to plan and schedule your project when contractors are not so busy. You'll find their prices 5-15 percent lower than during their peak season, you won't have to wait as long because they don't have as many projects on their books, and you'll find inventory from suppliers to be plentiful and discounted. Try to avoid spring remodeling season from late March through early June and fall remodeling from early September through Christmas. There is an abundance of activity during these time frames that may cause shortage of qualified craftsman and quality materials.

Another great time to remodel is when interest rates are low. By refinancing your home mortgage and accessing some of your equity, you'll not only get a great interest rate, but you'll be able to write off the interest. Check with your tax advisor for additional information.

If it's a pool or spa you want, try hiring a contractor during the off-season when nobody wants to swim. Because they have a desire to keep all of their employees working, they'll be flexible on their pricing. Hire them when everybody wants their pool done before Memorial Day and you're sure to pay a premium.

Deciding when to remodel is part of your planning process.

There are expensive and less-expensive times to hire a contractor. You'll get your best value by avoiding the busy seasons

Chapter 6

The Design Process

D o you need an architect? This can be determined based on the size of your project. If you're doing a simple, one-trade project such as French doors, a bay window, shutters, carpet, or painting, definitely not. If you're doing a major project such as a room addition which will require changes to your plumbing, electrical, or heating and cooling, and will alter the size and appearance of your home, most building departments will require that you obtain a building permit, and that an architect sign off on your plans. Not only will an architect help you with the design and budget, but also they'll make sure your project is designed in accordance with all applicable building codes and zoning regulations.

Most contractors don't want you to hire an architect. Their dislike is based on the fact that architects are a step up the power ladder. They act as a site supervisor, checking materials used and approve or disapprove workmanship before their client releases the next payment to the contractor.

This is exactly why you might consider hiring an architect for any large remodeling project. Besides providing aesthetic inspiration, architects provide detailed plans with specifics about materials and construction. Not surprisingly, bids prepared from architects' plans tend to be much closer to the actual final costs. Most architects generally charge 8-15 percent of a project budget, although some architects will review and critique plans for $100 per hour, usually with a minimum of $1,000.

On a small home improvement such as painting, a new door, moldings, or carpet, you're probably pretty well qualified to make some design decisions. You may have seen the work you desire at someone else's home, in a model home, on the Internet, or in a home magazine of some type. If you still feel uncomfortable, you may seek out an interior designer to assist you and help give you the necessary confidence to make a design decision.

However, most professional home improvement companies provide free design consultation and free bids by their employees. Rely on their expertise and experience to help put together the exact design you'll be happy with. But make sure the so-called expert/salesperson/designer that proposes working with you is really an expert. Sometimes an employee receives only two to three weeks of training by a sales manager or another salesman and may not only be of little help to you, but may possibly cause you headaches down the road because of their inexperience. If their employee hasn't been in this specific business a minimum of three years, his advice is of little value. Quite simply put, they are not an expert if they don't have the experience. So ask for someone in the home improvement company that has a minimum of three years experience with that company and with their specific products and services. Consulting and working with an expert will get you your best results.

The State of California requires all home improvement salespeople to be licensed. Ask to see their license to verify the validity, and make sure their license number is included on the contract/agreement.

Large projects may require the assistance of an architect

If you feel uncomfortable or insecure about making decisions, it may be time to consult a professional

Check on the education and experience of any professional before you hire him or her

Chapter 7

Finding the Right Contractor

Home improvement contractors hate to admit that getting into their industry can be no more difficult than printing up a business card. Virtually anyone with a truck, a few tools and a cell phone can call himself a contractor. No wonder botched home improvements have become one of the top sources of consumer complaints nationwide. So make sure you don't hire just anyone for your home improvement. You want to hire a legitimate qualified specialist. And you don't want to end up as a statistic.

As the contracting/home improvement industry evolves, homeowners continue to find an improved selection of specialized companies/contractors that are trade specific. The days of finding jack-of-all trades contractors that had a little bit of knowledge in many fields are almost gone. Today, the tradesmen have become specialists. Just as the medical field has multiple types of dentists and doctors, each an expert in their specialty field, the contracting industry has specialists who work in specific trades. Kitchen remodelers aren't door and window remodelers and vice versa. Rough construction framers are not finish carpenters, etc. If a guy can hang a door, it doesn't mean he can install a roof. If a company can build your deck, it doesn't mean they're qualified to build your room addition. Jack-of-all-trades, master of none, is a truism. You want to hire a company that does a specific trade every day, year round. Not a company that does a little of this, a little of that.

So, where do you find the right contractor? Your best bet is a qualified referral from someone who has done a similar project to yours. If they are happy with the quality and the service they received from their contractor, history will probably repeat itself and they should be a candidate for your job. However, you need to ask if the contractor showed up on time, if the job was finished on time, and if he returned calls promptly? Look at the workmanship yourself. Just because your neighbor was happy with the workmanship doesn't mean you will be satisfied. Question the sensitivity of the contractor to the living needs of the homeowner. Did he keep the jobsite clean and organized? Did the contractor willingly make any corrections, and did he seem concerned about resolving quality issues? You'll only find out if you ask, so don't be afraid to do so.

Yellow pages and newspaper advertising are another good source for finding a specialist for your home improvement. However, just because the ad is big, doesn't mean the contractor is good. They still need to be checked out thoroughly. Look closely at the advertisement. California requires all advertisements to include the contractor license number. If the ad omits the license number, they're already in violation of a basic contractor requirement. This could indicate the contractor hasn't been in business long, probably is not very experienced, and possibly is not qualified to work on your home. Take note of the contractor license number. Because the state issues license numbers in sequential order, the lower the number, the longer the contractor has been in business. You may also find good leads for qualified contractors from interior designers, architects, residential real estate agents, or a residential building inspector.

On your initial telephone call to a contractor's place of business or showroom, it would be unrealistic to expect an exact price on any project, whether it is shutters, or a new entry door. It's nearly impossible for the contractor to give accurate prices on a project he can't see. It is not fair to either of you to have him try and give you an exact price on a home improvement this way. There are measurements to take, a review of working conditions, confirmation of design, and a review of details to improve functionality and aesthetics. There are simply too many decisions that need to be made as part of the design that could make the project more or less expensive. Pressing for inaccurate prices will only cause disappointment for one or both parties. The best you can expect is a wide range "guesstimate" within 25-40 percent of the actual cost. Be patient and get an exact bid after all the details have been worked out.

Your first question is to find out exactly what they do so you can find out if the services or products they offer are really what you need. If you have a match, it's time to inquire how long the contractor has been in business. Business statistics show that 90 percent of all companies don't survive five years. In the contracting and home improvement industry, the percentage of failures is higher. Too often a carpenter or craftsman tries to be a businessman or entrepreneur. In reality, he's probably a great carpenter or craftsman, and knows nothing about running a business, insurance requirements, managing employees, handling finances, understanding accounting, or hiring and firing employees. When you hire someone that has not been in business a minimum of five years, don't plan on getting future warranty work completed that was promised at the time of sale. Most likely they'll be out of business.

Licensing is designed to protect the consumer from unqualified individuals, similar to a doctor or dentist needing a license to perform their respective work. The State of California requires a license for any contractor performing a job in which the total cost of the project is more than $500. Licensed contractors are then required to follow the contracting laws. If your project is larger than $500, you should call the Contractors State License Board at 1-800-321-CSLB (2752) to verify a license is valid and to investigate complaints against the license BEFORE you invite a contractor over to your home to give you a bid. There is no use wasting your time if the license is invalid or if there are multiple unresolved complaints. You may find some large home improvement companies have more complaints than small companies, due to the high volume of customers for whom they work. Most important, find out how they responded to their complaints and if their customers were ultimately satisfied with the outcome. However, there is a saying that "you can't please everybody", and this holds true in the home improvement industry.

Finding the Right Contractor

Avoid unlicensed contractors at all costs. They are a danger to your financial health because they expose you to significant financial risk. If an unlicensed contractor was working on your home and he did not have adequate bonding or insurance, in the event of a jobsite injury or property damage, the financial responsibilities become yours. Although an unlicensed contractor may give you a lower bid, because of the severe financial and legal consequences you may face, it simply isn't worth the risk. Always verify the contractor you hire is licensed and that the license he/she holds covers the work you want done.

The State of California also requires all contractors to have Workers Compensation and a Contractors License Bond. Visually verify that the contractor has both. You also need to ask if your city requires a business license to do work in your city. You could be exposed to city-mandated extras if the contractor is unfamiliar with your city.

If the contractor passes all these tests, it would be appropriate to visit his/her showroom or ask him/her to visit your home to discuss the home improvement project. They have now become a candidate for your project.

Be patient through the process. You'll be better off weeding through the amateurs while you look for your professional.

Find a contractor with experience doing exactly what you want to have done

Don't try to get a price quote or bid over the telephone, be patient and wait until all design criteria have been worked out

Verify status of Contractors' License before inviting a contractor to your home

Verify the contractor has Workman's Compensation Insurance and a Contractors License Bond

Be patient trying to find contractors to provide you bids

Chapter 8

The Bidding Process

Earlier, we established that it's imperative to get at least three bids and we worked through the process of finding the right contractor to bid the work. But what is a bid? How is it different from an estimate? And how do you collect bids?

A bid is an exact price provided by someone who has analyzed your precise drawings, provides precise drawings, or provides a very detailed written summary of exactly what it is being done on the project. This will enable them to determine the scope of the work and its costs. An estimate is just an estimate of the costs associated with the work description, and the real price could be higher or lower.

The best place to receive a bid is at your home, or wherever the work is being done. That way, it will be easy to discuss particulars, look at the actual areas where the work will be performed, and play "question and answer" in YOUR most comfortable setting. When receiving a bid, it must be in writing. If it's not in writing, it means nothing.

Once the contractors start coming to your home, explain to each of them as clearly as possible what you want to have done. Show them the research you've accumulated that pertains to your project. Make sure that you and each bidder really understand each other and all the details and expectations of the project. Be sure to listen with an open ear and try to get a sense of which contractors seem cooperative.

Many times, within the first meeting with a potential contractor, you'll get some hints about their professional or unprofessional approach to finding and managing home improvement projects. Was he on time for the meeting, or late without informing you he'd be late? Does he listen well, or does he interrupt often? Does he understand the local building codes? Does he malign other contractors or does he focus on the merits of himself and his company? Ask all your questions and listen closely.

During the interview process, ask to see the written warranty the contractor offers. Good contractors offer good warranties because they have confidence in the products and services they offer. It's probably not necessary to read the entire warranty at this early juncture of the process, but if the contractor does not have a written warranty for you to review, it indicates service and warranty work is low on their priorities. Remember, you pay for the warranty when you make the purchase, so you are entitled to a good one.

Keep in mind that not every contractor is on the lookout for unique ways to squeeze more money out of you. The best contractors will always suggest ways to save you money, perhaps by recommending ways to get quantity discounts or coming up with a design that looks a little different than the original plan, but eliminates some of the custom charges. These are qualities of an excellent contractor.

I realize that you may need to meet with more than three contractors to get three bids, but don't get impatient with the process and don't just start looking for anyone that can get to your home quickly. You may end up with the wrong contractor, the project may never get started, you may lose your deposit, the project may not meet building codes, and the job may not ever get done to your satisfaction. Be patient.

Beware if you get a bid from someone that can do the work immediately. If the contractor is not busy, there is probably a reason. If a contractor is very busy this should indicate their work is worth waiting for.

When you receive your bids from various contractors, the contractors must provide you with five specific documents that are required by the State of California regarding certain information relative to any contractual agreement regarding real property. The information is included on the original bid/proposal/agreement or in attachments to the agreement. They are:

1. California License Law Notice, explaining about the California Contractors License Law

2. Information about Commercial General Liability Insurance
3. Check Out Your Contractor, Check Out Your Contract
4. Notice to Owner explaining the California Mechanic's Lien Law
5. Notice of Cancellation explaining the procedure for canceling the agreement.

All five documents are printed at the end of this chapter.

If these documents are not given to you at the time the bid is presented, the contractor is not current with California requirements and should be excluded from consideration.

Get at least three bids for exactly what you want to have done at your home

Be patient through the entire bid process

Ask as many questions as you need to analyze the professionalism of the contractors

California License Law Notice

This form complies with professional standards in effect January 1-December 31, 2002

CALIFORNIA LAW REQUIRES US TO GIVE YOU THE FOLLOWING NOTICE:

"STATE LAW REQUIRES ANYONE WHO CONTRACTS TO DO CONSTRUCTION WORK TO BE LICENSED BY THE CONTRACTORS' STATE LICENSE BOARD IN THE LICENSE CATEGORY IN WHICH THE CONTRACTOR IS GOING TO BE WORKING---IF THE TOTAL PRICE OF THE JOB IS $500 OR MORE (INCLUDING LABOR AND MATERIALS).

"LICENSED CONTRACTORS ARE REGULATED BY LAWS DESIGNED TO PROTECT THE PUBLIC. IF YOU CONTRACT WITH SOMEONE WHO DOES NOT HAVE A LICENSE, THE CONTRACTORS' STATE LICENSE BOARD MAY BE UNABLE TO ASSIST YOU WITH A COMPLAINT. YOUR ONLY REMEDY AGAINST AN UNLICENSED CONTRACTOR MAY BE IN CIVIL COURT, AND YOU MAY BE LIABLE FOR DAMAGES ARISING OUT OF ANY INJURIES TO THE CONTRACTOR OR HIS OR HER EMPLOYEES.

"YOU MAY CONTACT THE CONTRACTOR'S STATE LICENSE BOARD TO FIND OUT IF THIS CONTRACTOR HAS A VALID LICENSE. THE BOARD HAS COMPLETE INFORMATION ON THE HISTORY OF LICENSED CONTRACTORS, INCLUDING ANY POSSIBLE SUSPENSIONS, REVOCATIONS, JUDGEMENTS, AND CITATIONS. THE BOARD HAS OFFICES THROUGHOUT CALIFORNIA. PLEASE CHECK THE GOVERNMENT PAGES OF THE WHITE PAGES FOR THE OFFICE NEAREST YOU OR CALL 1-800-321-CSLB FOR MORE INFORMATION."

X _____ X _____
     SIGNATURE   SIGNATURE

_____ **2002** _____ **2002**
      DATE   DATE

I'll Do It Differently Next Time. . .

Pursuant to Business & Professions Code Section §7159.3, contractors building single-family residences for owners who intend to occupy the home for at least a year must provide this notice and disclose whether or not they carry commercial general liability insurance.
This form complies with professional standards in effect January 1-December 31, 2002

✔ Information about Commercial General Liability Insurance

☐ **Did your contractor tell you whether he or she carries Commercial General Liability Insurance?**

Contractors building single-family residences for owners who intend to occupy the home for at least a year are required by law to tell you whether or not they carry Commercial General Liability Insurance. This written statement must accompany the contract.

☐ **What does this insurance cover?**

Commercial General Liability Insurance can protect against third-party bodily injury and accidental property damage. It is not intended to cover the work the contractor performs.

☐ **Is this insurance required?**

No. But the Contractors State License Board strongly recommends that all contractors carry it. The Board cautions you to evaluate the risk to your family and property when you hire a contractor who is not insured. Ask yourself if something went wrong, would this contractor be able to cover losses ordinarily covered by insurance?

☐ **How can you make sure the contractor is insured?**

If he or she is insured, the contractor is required by law to provide you with the name and telephone number of the insurance company. Check with the insurance company to verify that the contractor's insurance coverage will cover your project.

☐ **What about a contractor who is self-insured?**

A self-insured contractor has made a business decision to be personally responsible for losses that would ordinarily be covered by insurance. Before contracting with a self-insured contractor, ask yourself, if something went wrong, would this contractor be able to cover losses that should be covered by insurance?

For more information about Commercial General Liability Insurance, contact the **Contractors State License Board** at **www.cslb.ca.gov** or call **800-321-CSLB (2752).**

X _____   X _____
        Signature   Signature

_____ 2002   _____ 2002
        Date   Date

The Bidding Process

Pursuant to Business & Professions Code Section §7159.3, home improvement contractors building swimming pools must provide this notice. This form complies with professional standards in effect January 1-December 31, 2002

✓ Check Out Your Contractor

☐ Did you contact the Contractors State License Board (CSLB) to check the status of the contractor's license?
Contact the CSLB at 1-800-321-CSLB (2752) or visit our web site: www.cslb.ca.gov.

☐ Did you get at least (3) local references from the contractors you are considering?
Did you call them?

☐ Building permits-will the contractor get a permit before the work starts?

✓ Check Out The Contract

☐ Did you read and do you understand your contract?

☐ Does the three-day right to cancel a contract apply to you?
Contact the CSLB if you don't know.

☐ Does the contract tell you when work will start and end?

☐ Does the contract include a complete description of the work to be done, the material that will be used and equipment to be installed?
This description should include a plan and scale drawing showing the shape, size, dimensions and specifications. It should include brand names, model numbers, quantities and colors. Specific descriptions now will prevent disputes later.

☐ Are you required to pay a down payment?
The down payment for swimming pools should never be more than 2% of the contract price or $200, whichever is less.

☐ Is there a schedule of payments?
If there is a schedule of payments, you should pay only as work is completed and not before. There are some exceptions-contact the CSLB to find out what they are.

☐ Did your contractor give you a "Notice to Owner," a warning notice describing liens and ways to prevent them?
Even if you pay your contractor, a lien can be placed on your home by unpaid laborers, subcontractors, or material suppliers. A lien can result in you paying twice or, in some cases, losing your home in a foreclosure. Check the "Notice to Owner" for ways to protect yourself.

☐ Did you know changes or additions to your contract **must** be in writing?
Putting changes in writing reduces the possibility of a later dispute.

X _____   X _____
     Signature   Signature

_____ 2002   _____ 2002
        Date   Date

I'll Do It Differently Next Time. . .

NOTICE TO OWNER
REGARDING MECHANIC'S LIEN LAW
(COMPLIES WITH SECTION 7018.5 OF THE CALIFORNIA BUSINESS AND PROFESSIONS CODE)
This form complies with professional standards in effect January 1 - December 31, 2002

TO: FROM:

_____   _____
(OWNER NAME)   (CONTRACTOR NAME)

_____   _____
(STREET ADDRESS)   (STREET ADDRESS)

_____   _____
(CITY)   (STATE)   (ZIP)   (CITY)   (STATE)   (ZIP)

_____   _____
(TELEPHONE)   (FAX)   (TELEPHONE)   (FAX)

DESCRIPTION OF WORK OF IMPROVEMENT(WORK TO BE PERFORMED AT): _____

NOTICE TO OWNER

Under The California Mechanic's Lien Law any contractor, subcontractor, laborer, supplier or other person or entity who helps to improve your property, but is not paid for his/her work or supplies, has a right to place a lien on your home, land, or property where the work was performed and to sue you in court to obtain payment. This means that after a court hearing, your home, land, and property could be sold by a court officer and the proceeds of the sale used to satisfy what you owe. This can happen even if you have paid your contractor in full if the subcontractors, laborers or suppliers remain unpaid.

To preserve their right to file a claim or lien against your property, certain claimants such as subcontractors or material suppliers are each required to provide you with a document called a "Preliminary Notice." Contractors and laborers who contract with owners directly do not have to provide such notice since you are aware of their existence as an owner. A preliminary notice is not a lien against your property. Its purpose is to notify you of persons or entities that may have a right to file a lien against your property if they are not paid. In order to perfect their lien rights, a contractor, subcontractor, supplier, or laborer must file a mechanic's lien with the county recorder which then becomes a recorded lien against your property. Generally, the maximum time allowed for filing a mechanic's lien against your property is 90 days after substantial completion of your project.

TO INSURE EXTRA PROTECTION FOR YOURSELF AND YOUR PROPERTY, YOU MAY WISH TO TAKE ONE OR MORE OF THE FOLLOWING STEPS:

1. Require that your contractor supply you with a payment and performance bond (not a license bond), which provides that the bonding company will either complete the project or pay damages up to the amount of the bond. This payment and performance bond as well as a copy of the construction contract should be filed with the county recorder for your further protection. The payment and performance bond will usually cost from 1 to 5 percent of the contract amount depending on the contractor's bonding ability. If a contractor cannot obtain such bonding, it may indicate his or her financial incapacity.
2. Require that payments be made directly to subcontractors and material suppliers through a joint control. Funding services may be available, for a fee, in your area which will establish voucher or other means of payment to your contractor. These services may also provide you with lien waivers and other forms of protection. Any joint control agreement should include the addendum approved by the registrar.
3. Issue joint checks for payment, made out to both your contractor and subcontractors or material suppliers involved in the project. The joint checks should be made payable to the persons or entities which send preliminary notices to you. These persons or entities have indicated that they may have lien rights on your property, therefore you need to protect yourself. This will help to insure that all persons due payment are actually paid.
4. Upon making payment on any completed phase of the project, and before making any further payments, require your contractor to provide you with unconditional "Waiver and Release" forms signed by each material supplier, subcontractor and laborer involved in that portion of the work for which payment was made. The statutory lien releases are set forth in exact language in Section 3262 of the Civil Code. Most stationery stores will sell the "Waiver and Release" forms if your contractor does not have them. The material suppliers, subcontractors, and laborers that you obtain release from are those persons or entities who have filed preliminary notices with you. If you are not certain of the material suppliers, subcontractors, and laborers working on your project, you may obtain a list from your contractor. On projects involving improvements to a single family residence or a duplex owned by individuals, the persons signing these releases lose the right to file a mechanic's lien claim against your property. In other types of construction, this protection may still be important, but may not be complete.

To protect yourself under this option, you must be certain that all material suppliers, subcontractors, and laborers have signed the "Waiver and Release" form. If a mechanics' lien has been filed against your property, it can only be voluntarily released by a recorded "Release of Mechanics' Lien" signed by the person or entity that filed the mechanics' lien against your property unless the lawsuit to enforce the lien was not timely filed. You should not make any final payments until any and all such liens are removed. **YOU SHOULD CONSULT AN ATTORNEY IF A LIEN IS FILED AGAINST YOUR PROPERTY.**

METHOD OF TRANSMITTAL:

☐U.S. Mail   ☐First Class   ☐Certified   ☐FAX/Phone # _____
☐Federal Express   ☐Personal Delivery.

CONTRACTOR: _____   OWNER: **X**
_____/02_____   _____
(DATE)   (DATE)

The Bidding Process

"NOTICE OF CANCELLATION"
This form complies with professional standards in effect January 1 - December 31, 2002

_____ **/02**
(Date of Transaction)

You may cancel this transaction, without any penalty or obligation, within three business days from the above date.

If you cancel, any property traded, in any payments made by you under the contract or sale, and any negotiable instrument executed by you will be returned within 10 days following receipt by the seller of your cancellation notice, and any security interest arising out of the transaction will be canceled.

If you cancel, you must make available to the seller at your residence, in substantially as good condition as when received, any goods delivered to you under this contract or sale, or you may, if you wish, comply with the instructions of the seller regarding the return shipment of the goods at the seller's expense and risk.

If you do make the goods available to the seller and the seller does not pick them up them up within 20 days of the date of your notice of cancellation, you may retain or dispose of the goods without any further obligation. If you fail to make the goods available to the seller, or if you agree to return the goods to the seller and fail to do so, then you remain liable for performance of all obligations under the contract

To cancel this transaction, mail or deliver a signed and dated copy of this cancellation notice, or any other written notice, or send a telegram to

_____
(Name of Seller)

at

_____
(Address of Sellers Place of Business)

not later than midnight of

_____
(Date)

I hereby cancel this transaction

_____ **/ / 2002**
(Date)

X _____
(Buyer's Signature)

I (we each) acknowledge receipt of two copies of this form.

Buyer: **X** _____   Buyer: **X** _____

Chapter 9

Selecting the Right Contractor

By now you should have three bids, and it's time to make the commitment to one of them.

First, did you check out the references on completed projects from all three contractors? Most references are glad to discuss their experiences. They were once in your shoes and probably how know you feel. If possible, try to see the finished work and ask questions about the contractor's performance. Did he start and finish the project as stated in his contract? Was he organized and did he keep the area around the project clean? Are his crews well mannered, trustworthy, and professional? Did he live up to his responsibilities of the contract?

Second, don't get carried away with bargain hunting. Super low bids don't mean better anything. Renegades running their business out of a post office box are cheaper, but riskier. A low bidder may have misinterpreted your plans, or he is not including all the work bid by his competitors. He may be desperate to land your job to keep his business afloat and get cash flow, or he may be planning to pad his bill with change orders (an addendum to the contract) once work gets started. Remember, the bitterness of poor workman-ship lasts much longer than the sweetness of a low price, and if a bid sounds too good to be true, it probably is.

Third, keep in mind that contractors need to make a living. They have families to support, health insurance requirements, tool and vehicle expenses and overhead. They need vacations, have mort-gages, and someday they'll want to retire, just like you and I. To do this they need to, and deserve to, make a fair profit if they do the job correctly. Remember also that you want the contractor you hire to have well trained, qualified employees and they need and deserve all of the above benefits as well. The best workman will require good pay, just like a professional in any business. Be willing to pay for quality, and then demand that you get it.

So how do you make a conclusive decision? Which contractor understood your expectations best? Which contractor gave you the best first impression? Which contractor best represented his company in a professional manner? Which contractor provides the best warranty? Whose quality was most impressive? Which contractor gave the most believable presentation about the virtues of his company? Most likely your gut is pushing you toward a favorite. Trust your gut, it's probably right.

> Check out references thoroughly
>
> Beware of low prices
>
> It's okay for a contractor to make a profit
>
> Trust your gut

Chapter 10

Permits

Most cities require a permit for any electrical or plumbing work, a sprinkler system, replacement doors and windows, a new roof, and most other home improvements other than painting, carpet, shutters, and molding work. A building permit is always required whenever structural work is involved, or when the basic living area of a home is changed. Your bids should include any costs associated with work being performed to meet all applicable building codes. Keep in mind that building codes only set minimum safety standards; they do not protect you against poor quality work.

The contractor should obtain the necessary building permits. This should be spelled out in your contract, otherwise, you may be held legally responsible for failure to obtain the required permits. Permits are to be pulled prior to the work starting, but some contractors start work without them. Why? Depending on how efficient your local bureaucrats are, it can sometimes take weeks to issue a basic permit. Getting plans approved by a co-op, condo board, a homeowners association, or, heaven forbid, a landmark or coastal commission, can take even longer. Be patient, play by the rules, insist that permits are pulled before work starts.

Some homeowners choose to avoid permits, as well as the expense, and delays associated with them. Bad idea. The home-owner is legally and financially responsible if the infraction is discovered. And run, don't walk, from any contractor who asks you to get the permit because the person that pulls the permit is considered to be the contractor and is liable if the work does not comply with the building codes.

The permit for your job, along with the project plans and specifications, must be posted at the jobsite before work begins. Check to make sure this happens.

Be aware of permit requirements

Let the permits be the responsibility of the contractor

Chapter 11

Controlling and Protecting Your Money

Now that you've decided on whom you want to do the work for you, and you know how much it's going to cost, let's plan out a strategy on paying for the project. Obviously, you'll want to protect your money and reduce your risk.

Most homeowners take on the responsibility of coming up with their own money for their project either through a home equity loan, a second mortgage from their bank or credit union, or by tapping a savings account. Some home improvement contractors can arrange financing for their customers through home improvement lenders or through utility company financing, but generally, consumers can get the best rates on loans through their own bank or credit union where they already have established credit.

When a loan is secured by your home equity, the interest paid can help reduce your taxes. Talk with your C.P.A. or financial adviser for the tax ramifications. No other loans will provide you those benefits.

Many home improvement companies will offer you ninety days, 180 days, or one year same as cash financing. Although this sounds like a great offer, someone is paying the interest for the specified time period, and that someone is you. The use of money is not free, so the interest costs are packed into the price you pay for the job. When same as cash financing is offered to you, and you decline the offer, you will have room to negotiate on the bid by approximately 1 percent for each thirty days of same as cash financing. If 180 days same as cash is offered, the contractor probably has about 6 percent packed into his price. Negotiate with him for that discount.

If you cannot pay for a project without a loan of some type, and if you have not previously secured the financing, it is a good idea to add a clause to your contract allowing you to cancel the contract at any time if you cannot secure financing at an agreeable interest rate. This way you are not obligated should you not be able to secure a fair loan.

When deciding among your loan options, you need to ask if there are pre-payment penalties. Pre-payment penalties enable a lender to capture a portion of their earnings and cover their expenses should you pay the loan off early, sell your home and move, or unexpectedly come into some money. With some loans, the pre-payment penalty is very, very expensive and needs to be considered.

One of the biggest errors homeowners make in a home improvement project is paying the contractor too much money too fast. Many contractors will ask for a 25-50 percent down payment to start a project. In California, the down payment for home improvements must not exceed $1,000 or 10 percent of the contract amount, whichever is less, unless the contractor has secured a performance bond (see Chapter 12) which guarantees completion of the project. On a contract for a swimming pool, the maximum down payment is $200 or 2 percent of the contract amount, whichever is less. There are no exceptions for special order materials. The deposit money you are giving him may be going to fund another project he is working on, or to pay off a supplier on another project. Never, ever give a contractor a bigger deposit than the law allows. It is a risk you don't want to take.

Home improvement contracts should include a schedule of progress payments showing the dollar amount of payments specifically referenced to the amount of work or services to be performed, or any materials and equipment to be supplied. Payments should not exceed the value of the work performed, except the initial down payment, NO MATTER WHAT. If the contractor gets ahead of you on the money versus the work performed, you are at risk. If a contractor wants more money than the work he has performed, it's a sure sign that he needs cash flow to finish up other projects, or he may have personal financial issues he's dealing with, kind of like the "rob Peter to pay Paul" scenario. A qualified contractor has established credit with suppliers and should not need your money to do the project. Remember, who ever has the money is in control. Don't fall for a sob story about his need for extra money exceeding the work he has completed. It is a danger sign, a financial warning, and is cause for alarm.

A great way to lay out the progress payments is to have payments coincide with milestones of the job. This is something to discuss with the contractor and should be a negotiating point. One of the milestones that can be used multiple times is based on the successful passing of inspections by city inspectors. Get an inspection passed, pay some money.

Another way to control the money, especially on big home improvements or remodeling, is to use a funding control company to disburse contract payments. A fund control company is basically a licensed escrow company that specializes in construction. Instead of giving the money to your contractor, you give it to the funding control company, and they make the payments to the contractor, sub-contractor, or companies that supplied labor or materials for your project.

Funding control companies will make checks and balances prior to making progress payments, but they are not required or to be expected to see that work is completed or materials supplied. They typically use vouchers as authorization to pay the contractor based on bills presented by the contractor. The vouchers should be treated like checks and only signed by you, and used as each phase of the project is completed.

For more protection, insist that the funding control company use an "Addendum to Control Agreement/Escrow Instructions." You, your contractor, and a representative of the funding control company would sign this addendum. This will allow a method of making payments designed to protect your money and property. The company should also make onsite inspections as its way to verify any work or materials it pays for have been provided.

When looking for a funding control company, check with your lender or contractor for a referral. For just a small percentage of the contract price, a qualified, reputable funding control company will eliminate or reduce your risks on the project.

All payments to your contractor should be by check, money order, or credit card. Never pay with cash.

Interest free loans are not really free

Beware of loans with pre-payment penalties

Do not give more of a deposit than required by law

Your contract should have progress payments coinciding with work performed

Consider a funding control company on a large home improvement or remodel

Chapter 12

Bonding Is Important

There are many different types of bonds used in contracting home improvements. In this chapter, I'll review the most common bonds and their purposes.

Contractors License Bond

In California, each licensed contractor must have a license bond with the Contractors State License Board. It is generally a $5,000 bond with a surety company or a cash deposit of $5,000 to the state. This type of bond is not a guarantee of performance, competence, or financial responsibility for the contractor. If the contractor goes out of business and does not complete your project, or those of his other customers, multiple claims will be made to the $5,000 bond and all claimants will split the $5,000. This type of bond is not very good at protecting you in case your contractor goes out of business or leaves town in the middle of the project.

Payment and Completion Bond/ Performance Bond

These types of bonds guarantee that the project will get completed according to the building plans and specifications EVEN if your contractor abandons the job or the work is unacceptable. In that situation, the bonding company will hire another contractor to complete the work or they will negotiate a settlement for damages. For this type of protection, you would ask your contractor to obtain the bond in the amount of the contract price. This should be recognized as part of the cost of doing business. This type of bond generally costs approximately 2 percent of the contract amount. It is an excellent insurance policy and provides complete protection. Large jobs financed by lenders generally require this type of bond for everyone's protection.

You should understand that when you require this type of bond, it excludes a newer contracting business, or a financially unstable contractor, from bidding on your project. Contractors must be strong financially, have a proven track record, and practice sound business techniques to obtain this type of bond. If a contractor cannot obtain this bond, or is unwilling to obtain this bond, this is a strong signal that the contractor cannot qualify for some reason. That's okay. Find one that can if you feel you need this protection and assurance. There are plenty of great contractors that qualify for the bond and you'll be better off with a professional than an amateur.

Contract Bond
This bond guarantees both job completion and payment for all labor and materials.

All home improvement contracts must contain a notice that says the owner has the right to require the contractor to have a

Bonding Is Important

performance and payment bond for their protection. This notice is in the "Notice to Owner" section of your agreement.

A Contractors License Bond does not provide much financial protection

There are bonds available for purchase that provide financial protection, especially on large home improvements

Chapter 13

The Agreements, Contract, and Paperwork

Properly written contracts supplied by the contractor are essential. In California, any home improvement over $500 must be written into a contract. If it is a dreaded "time and materials" contract it must be in writing with a fixed price, if it is anticipated that the cost might exceed $500.

A California home improvement contract must include the following:

1. Contractor's name, address, and license number
2. Notice to owner
3. Notice required by diciplined contractors
4. Commencement of work and completion statement
5. Description of work
6. Change order procedure
7. Schedule of payments
8. Arbitration notice
9. Notice of right to cancel
10. Notice required for a lien contract

If the contract does not include these ten items, for your own protection, do not sign the contract. The law requires all listed items, and licensed contractors need to abide.

Obviously, a printed contract form obtained at the stationary store does not provide the legalese required and will demonstrate that whomever presented this to you is unqualified. These types of contracts are illegal for a licensed contractor to use.

At the end of this chapter, I have included an example of a contract that complies with Section 7159 of the California Business and Professional Code.

Besides the ten items required by the State of California, the contract must specify the exact work you want done. No vagueness, only exactness. That way, both parties know exactly what is going to be done and what is not going to be done. It should also include a detailed description or drawing of the project, possibly an architect's or engineer's drawings attached to the contract, and a complete list of the exact materials to be used. It is your responsibility to insist that this is specified. If you don't, it is likely that the contractor will not provide this information.

In addition, make sure the agreement includes everything you feel is important to the job, including complete clean-up and removal of debris and excess materials, and any special requests you may have, such as saving excess lumber for firewood or saving certain material that you think you may want to re-use or recycle. Also include instructions on which bathrooms may be used, where to store materials, your concerns for pets and children, etc. The more details you include and communicate in writing, the better off both parties will be.

Never assume anything about this transaction. Get as many things that are important to you as possible in writing. If permits are necessary and required, it should be written into the contract. Read and understand the agreements on design, materials, change orders, supplier of products, and who will do the work, BEFORE you sign any paperwork at all.

A common schedule-saver is to insert a late clause in your contract of $100 to $1,000 per day when the contractor is late on completion of the project or is procrastinating for some reason. However, a smart contractor will want an early completion clause with a $100 to $1,000 premium per day if he gets the job done before the completion date. If time is of the essence, this may need to be written into the agreement.

Any home improvement over $500 must be written in a contract

An agreement must include all the specifics of exactly what you want done

Get everything in writing, no exceptions

HOME IMPROVEMENT CONTRACT

(Complies with Section 7159 of California Business and Professions Code, as amended)
This form complies with professional standards in effect January 1-December 31, 2002

THIS AGREEMENT BETWEEN:

_____	_____
(Contractor's Name)	(Owner's Name)
_____	_____
(Contractor's License Number)	(Owner's Home Address)
_____	_____
(Contractor's Address)	(City, State & Zip)
_____	_____
(City, State & Zip)	(Owner's Business Address)
_____	_____
(Telephone-FAX)	(City, State & Zip)

CONSTRUCTION LENDER: Name and address of construction fund holder is:

_____
(Name And Branch Address Of Bank, Savings And Loan Assn., Escrow, Agent, Joint Control Or Other)

DESCRIPTION OF PROJECT (including materials and equipment to be used or installed): Contractor will furnish all labor, materials and equipment to construct in a good workmanlike manner (Describe Labor, Materials, And Equipment To Be Furnished):

WORK TO BE PERFORMED AT (Legal Description And Street Address If Known):

TIME FOR COMPLETION: The work to be performed by Contractor pursuant to this Agreement shall be commenced within _____ (_____) days from this date or approximately on (Date): _____ and shall be substantially completed within _____ (_____) days or approximately on (Date): _____
Commencement of work shall be defined as (Briefly Describe Type Of Work Representing Commencement):

Contractor's failure to substantially commence work without lawful excuse, within twenty (20) days from the date specified above is a violation of the Contractors License Law.
PAYMENT: Owner agrees to pay contractor a total cash price of $_____ Down payment (if any) $_____
(By California law cannot exceed $1,000.00 or 10% of contract price, which ever is lesser.)
Should contract call for a salesman's commission to be paid out of contract price, said payment shall be made by dispersing party to the contractor, per Section 7159(3).

Payment schedule as follows:	WHEN		WHEN
$ _____	_____	$ _____	_____
$ _____	_____	$ _____	_____
$ _____	_____	$ _____	_____

Upon satisfactory payment being made for any portion of the work performed, the contractor shall, prior to any further payment being made furnish to the person contracting for the home improvement or swimming pool a full and unconditional release from any claim or mechanic's lien pursuant to Section 3114 of the California Civil Code, for that portion of the work for which payment has been made.
ALLOWANCES: The following items or specific prices as indicated are included in the contract price as allowances. The contract price shall be adjusted upward / downward based upon actual amounts rather than estimated amounts herein _____

TERMS AND CONDITIONS: The terms and conditions attached are expressly incorporated into this Agreement.
You, the buyer, may cancel this transaction at any time prior to midnight of the third business day after the date of this transaction. Or if this is a contract for the repair of damages resulting from an earthquake, flood, fire, hurricane, riot, storm, tidal wave, or other similar catastrophic occurrence for which a state of emergency has been declared, you the buyer may cancel this transaction at any time prior to midnight of the seventh business day after the date of this transaction. Any questions concerning a contractor may be referred to the Registrar, Contractor's State License Board, P.O. Box 26000, Sacramento, California 95826 or call 1-800-321-CSLB for more information. See the attached notice of cancellation form for an explanation of this right.

Firm Name: _____	Date: _____, **2002** _____	
(Contractor's Firm Name, If Any)		

Name and State Registration Number of any salesman who solicited or negotiated this contract.

By: _____ Signature: _____
(Contractor Or Agent Sign Here)

Owner: **X** _____ Date: _____

Owner: **X** _____ Date: _____
(If More Than One Owner, Please Sign Here)

TERMS AND CONDITIONS

1. Permits and Licenses
Subcontractor shall obtain and pay for permits and licenses governing the Subcontractor's specific work in sufficient time to allow uninterrupted progress of this work and that of others.

2. Extra Work
Subcontractor shall provide in a good and workmanlike manner only that labor and materials specified herein. Additional work not specified in this agreement will be provided only upon written authorization of Contractor. Payment for such additional work shall be provided in accordance with the Terms of Payment specified herein. In the event that there are unit prices for the original scope of work or the extra work, then the extra work shall be at an identical unit price to the original scope of work.
In the event of an emergency condition, the General Contractor's job supervisor may authorize the extra work. In any event, a signed change order covering the emergency work shall be executed by the parties within 48 hours afer the extra work is completed.

3. Labor and Material Releases
Subcontractor shall provide satisfactory proof of payment in the form of labor and material releases covering work for each payment applied for and received from Contractor. Such releases provided by Subcontractor are only valid and conditioned upon receipt by Subcontractor of lawful U.S. currency for full amount of said payment.

4. Extra Time
Time is of the essence of this agreement. Subcontractor agrees to start work within 72 hours of proper notification by the Contractor and to diligently pursue work through to completion. Subcontractor shall not be responsible for delays incurred as a result of acts of neglect or omission of Owner, Owner's employees or agent, Contractor, Contractor's employees or agents, other subcontractors, acts of God, stormy or inclement weather, strikes, lockouts, boycotts, or other union activities, extra work ordered by Contractor, acts of public enemy, riots or civil commotion, inability to secure material through regular recognized channels, imposition of government priority or allocation of materials, failure of Contractor to provide payments when due, or delays caused by inspections, or changes ordered by the inspectors of governmental bodies concerned, or other causes beyond control of Subcontractor.

5. Indemnity
All of the work performed at the site of construction or in preparing or delivering materials or equipment to the site shall be at the risk of Subcontractor exclusively. Subcontractor shall indemnify and hold Contractor harmless from any claim, liability, loss, damage, cost, expense, including reasonable attorney's fees, award, fine or judgment with respect to or arising out of the work, including without limitation, any such claims, liability, loss, damage, cost, expense, award, fine or judgement arising by reason of death or bodily injury to persons, injury to property, defects in workmanship or materials, or design defects (if the design originated with Subcontractor), or arising by reason of Contractor's alleged or actual negligent act or omission, regardless of whether such act or omission is active or passive. Subconctractor shall not be obligated to indemnify Contractor with respect to the sole negligence or willful misconduct of Contractor, its agents or servants or other subcontractors who are directly responsible to Contractor.

6. Insurance
Subcontractor shall carry, at Subcontractor's expense, Worker's Compensation insurance convering all Subcontractor's employees and public liability and property damage insurance covering Subcontractor's liability in the minimum amount of $300,000 unless specified otherwise.

Subcontractor shall also carry automobile public liability and property damage insurance in an amount agreeable to Contractor.

Prior to commencement of work, Subcontractor agrees to provide to Contractor certificates of such coverage upon request of Contractor. Subcontractor agrees to maintain said insurance in full force and effect during the construction herein. In the event that Subcontractor does not provide said insurance, or said insurance shall for any reason lapse, then General Contractor may purchase said insurance and charge Subcontractor therefor.

7. Bonding of Subcontractor.
Concurrently with the execution of this agreement or any time during its performance, Subcontractor shall, if required by Contractor, execute a Labor Material Bond and Faithful Performance Bond in an amount equal to one-hundred percent (100%) of the contract price. Said bonds shall be executed by a corporate surety acceptable to Contractor and shall be in a form satisfactory to Contractor.

8. Work Stoppage
Subcontractor shall have the right to stop work if payments are not made when due. If the work shall be stopped under an order of any court or other authority, or by Owner, or Contractor for a period of sixty (60) days, without the fault of the Subcontractor, then Subcontractor may, at Subcontractor's option, upon five (5) days written notice, demand and receive payment for all work executed and materials supplied including an amount for overhead and profit, proportionate to the work completed.

9. Guarantee
Unless otherwise specified, Subcontractor guarantees that all materials fabricated or furnished by Subcontractor will be a standard quality, free from defects, and will be installed or applied in a good and workmanlike manner. Such labor and materials guaranteed for a period of one-year when subject to normal use and care, and provided Contractor has complied in full with payments and all terms and conditions of this contract. Specified assemblies or units purchased by Subcontractor which are included in this agreement are provided subject to the manufactuer's or distributor's guarantee or warranty and not that of Subcontractor. THIS IS IN LIEU OF ALL GUARANTEES EXPRESSED OR IMPLIED.

10. Clean-up
Subcontractor agrees to keep the premises in a neat and safe condition and at the end of Subcontractor's performance (or each day), Subcontractor shall leave the premises in neat broom-clean condition.

11. Arbitration
If at any time any controversy shall arise between Subcontractor and Contractor with respect to any matter in question arising out of, or related to, this agreement or the breach thereof, which the parties do not properly adjust and determine, said controversy shall be decided by arbitration administered by and in accordance with the Construction Industry Arbitration Rules of the American Arbitration Association then obtaining unless the parties mutually agree otherwise. This agreement so to arbitrate shall be specifically enforceable under the prevailing arbitration law. The award rendered by the abitrators shall be final, and judgment may be entered upon it in any court having jurisdiction thereof. Administrative fees as described by the American Arbitration Association shall be advanced one half by each party. However, in the event that the dispute between the parties is less than $5,000, then either party may choose to litigate the matter in the Small Claims Courts and the agreement to arbitrate shall not be binding. The prevailing party in any dispute shall be entitled to its reasonable costs including attorney's fees.

I'll Do It Differently Next Time. . .

NOTICE TO OWNER

"Under the California Mechanics' Lien Law, any contactor, subcontractor, laborer, supplier, or other person or entity who helps to improve your property, but is not paid for his or her work or supplies, has a right to place a lien on your home, land, or property where the work was performed and to sue you in court to obtain payment.

This means that after a court hearing, your home, land, and property could be sold by a court officer and the proceeds of the sale used to satisfy what you owe. This can happen even if you have paid your contractor in full if the contractor's subcontractors, laborers, or suppliers remain unpaid.

To preserve their rights to file a claim or lien against your property, certain claimants such as subcontractors or material suppliers are each required to provide you with a document called a "Preliminary Notice." Contractors and laborers who contract with owners directly do not have to provide such notice since you are aware of their existence as an owner. A preliminary notice is not a lien against your property if they are not paid. In order to perfect their lien rights, a contractor, subcontractor, supplier, or laborer must file a mechanics'' lien with the county recorder which then becomes a recorded lien against your property. Generally, the maximum time allowed for filing a mechanics' lien against your property is 90 days after substantial completion of your project.

TO INSURE EXTRA PROTECTION FOR YOURSELF AND YOUR PROPERTY, YOU MAY WISH TO TAKE
ONE OF THE FOLLOWING STEPS:

(1) Require that your contractor supply you with a payment and performance bond (not a license bond), which provides that the bonding company will either complete the project or pay damages up to the amount of the bond. This payment and performance bond as well as a copy of the construction contract should be filed with the county recorder for your further protection. The payment and performance bond will usually cost from 1 to 5 percent of the contract amount depending on the contractor's bonding ability. If a contractor cannot obtain such bonding, it may indicate his or her financial incapacity.

(2) Require that payments be made directly to subcontractors and material suppliers through a joint control. Funding services may be available, for a fee, in your area which will establish voucher or other means of payment to your contractor. These services may also provide you with lien waivers and other forms of protection. Any joint control agreement should include the addendum approved by the registrar.

(3) Issue joint checks for payment, made out to both your contractor and subcontractors or material suppliers involved in the project. The joint checks should be made payable to the persons or entities which send preliminary notices to you. Those persons or entities have indicated that they may have lien rights on your property, therefore you need to protect yourself. This will help to insure that all persons due payment are actually paid.

(4) Upon making payment on any completed phase of the project, and before making any further payments, require your contractor to provide you with unconditional "Waiver and Release" forms signed by each material supplier, subcontractor, and laborer involved in that portion of the work for which payment was made. The statutory lien releases are set forth in exact language in Section 3262 of the Civil Code. Most stationery stores will sell the "Waiver and Release" forms if your contractor does not have them. The material suppliers, subcontractors, and laborers that you obtain releases from are those persons or entities who have filed preliminary notices with you. If you are not certain of the material suppliers, subcontractors, and laborers working on your project, you may obtain a list from your contractor. On projects involving improvements to a single-family residence or a duplex owned by the individuals, the persons signing these releases lose the right to file a mechanics' lien claim against your property. In other types of construction, this protection may still be important, but may not be as complete.

To protect yourself under this option, you must be certain that all material suppliers, subcontractors, and laborers have signed the "Waiver and Release" form. If a mechanics' lien has been filed against your property, it can only be voluntarily released by a recorded "Release of Mechanics' Lien" signed by the person or entity that filed the mechanics' lien against your property unless the lawsuit to enforce the lien was not timely filed. You should not make any final payments until any and all such liens are removed. You should consult an attorney if a lien is filed against your property."

Chapter 14

Canceling the Contract

Sometimes, after you've signed an agreement, you may change your mind for a number of reasons. Whatever the reason doesn't matter. There are various cancellation provisions with which you need to be familiar. These are outlined in this chapter.

The first is "The Home Solicitation Act." This allows you to cancel the contract within three business days after signing, if the transaction occurs in your home or away from "appropriate trade premises." To cancel, you need only to give the contractor a signed and dated copy of the "Notice of Cancellation" (see document at the end of this chapter) that the contractor gave you at the time of purchase. If the contractor did not give you the "Notice of Cancellation" form at the time of purchase, you may cancel the agreement at anytime. In this case, the three-day cancellation period would not be a factor because the contractor has not complied, and the cancellation period will not begin until he has complied. The cancellation provisions are most commonly applied to sales made in the buyer's home, but the test is "whether the contract offer is made somewhere other than the seller's place of business."

There are other circumstances that may extend the cancellation period past three days. The contract must be in writing and must be in the same language used in the oral presentation. The contractor must give you a copy of the contract and "Notice of Cancellation." The contract must be dated and signed by the buyer, and must state on the first page the name and address of the contractor to which the "Notice of Cancellation" is to be sent. It must also include the date the buyer signed the contract.

In addition, the contract must contain this statement in bold near the space for the buyers signature:
"YOU, THE BUYER, MAY CANCEL THIS TRANSACTION AT ANY TIME PRIOR TO MIDNIGHT OF THE THIRD BUSINESS DAY AFTER THE DATE OF THIS TRANSACTION. SEE ATTACHED NOTICE OF CANCELLATION FORM FOR AN EXPLAINATION OF THE RIGHT. IF YOU CANCEL AFTER THE CANCELLATION PERIOD, YOU WILL BE RESPONSIBLE FOR LIQUIDATED DAMAGES.

A "business day" is referred to as a calendar day, but excludes Sundays and holidays.

If the contractor has not complied with any of the requirements described above, the buyer may cancel the contract "at anytime" until the contractor has complied with those requirements. A buyer who decides to cancel does not need to use the "Notice of Cancellation" form provided by the contractor. A buyer can simply express in writing his desire not to be bound by the contract and send it to the address specified in the agreement. If sent by mail, the notice of cancellation is effective when deposited in the mail, properly addressed, with postage prepaid. A cancellation notice may also be sent by telegram to the contractor's address.

There are a couple of important exceptions to the Home Solicitation Sales Act. When contracts for emergency repairs or services are written which are necessary for the immediate protection of people or property, where the buyer initiates the contract and gives the contractor a signed and dated personal statement describing the situation, a buyer can waive the right to cancel. (See the "Waiver of Right to Cancel" at the end of this chapter)

Another exception involves transactions that are subject to rescission under the Truth in Lending Act. If the home improvement is to be financed and involves a security interest in the buyers home, the Truth in Lending Act's three-business day right of rescission (cancellation) probably applies. The Truth in Lending rescission right arises in a consumer credit transaction, where a non-purchase lien or security interest is taken in the consumers principal dwelling, or where a security interest in the dwelling may arise by operation of law (e.g., a mechanics' or material man's lien). The credit must be extended to a natural person for personal, family, or household purposes, by a creditor who regularly extends consumer credit (this can be a contractor or lender). Major exceptions to the rescission provisions include loans to finance the construction or purchase of a home, and refinancings of the same property by the same creditor with no new advance of funds.

Business and Professions Code Section 7163 complements and supplements the Truth in Lending Act's rescission provision described above. Cancellation after the three-day rescission may be allowed if any of these three situations arise:

1. **If the obtaining of a loan for all, or a portion, of the contract price for a home improvement contract is a condition precedent to the contract**
2. **If the contractor provides financing or helps the buyer in any manner to obtain a loan**
3. **If the contractor refers the buyer to a lender or to any person for the purposes of arranging a loan**

If **one** of these conditions is present, the contract is not enforceable against the buyer unless **all** of the following requirements are satisfied:

1. **The third party, if any, agrees to make the loan**
2. **The buyer agrees to accept the loan or financing**
3. **The buyer does not rescind the loan or financing transaction, as permitted by the Truth in Lending Act, if that Act's provisions are applicable**

In general, the buyer's waiver of rights under California Business & Practice Section 7163 is void and unenforceable.

A waiver is permitted, however, to the extent that the contract is for emergency repairs or services that are necessary for the immediate protection of people or property. In this situation, the buyer must give the contractor a signed and dated personal statement which describes the emergency, states that the contractor has informed the buyer of the buyer's right to cancel under B & P Section 7163, and states that the buyer waives those rights.

Each owner of the property must sign the waiver. Waivers on printed forms are void and unenforceable.

California Business & Practice Section 7165 allows use of substitute provisions in the case of a swimming pool contract financed by a third-party lender.

After signing the contract, use the next two days to review the contract and paperwork again to make sure you've covered all your needs and requirements on this project. If something bothers you, discuss it with the contractor. If you still feel uncomfortable, cancel the contract. You can still re-hire the same contractor after you get the issues clear in your mind and in writing after you've canceled. Simply sign a new contract with whatever changes you omitted on the first contract. If you can't work out the problems with your original contractor, get a different contractor.

No matter what, don't get caught with a contractor that pressured you into an order that you feel uncomfortable with, or you felt hurried or pushed into. Make sure you're 100 percent comfortable before proceeding. You only want to do this home improvement once.

You have the right to cancel the contract, but most often, it must be done within three business days

If the contract does not meet certain criteria, you may be able to cancel the agreement at any time

You may waive your right to cancel for emergency repairs

Canceling the Contract

"NOTICE OF CANCELLATION"

This form complies with professional standards in effect January 1 - December 31, 2002

Following an earthquake, flood, fire, hurricane, riot, storm, tidal wave, or other similar catastrophic occurrence.

_____ **/02**
(Date of Transaction)

     You may cancel this transaction, without any penalty or obligation, within seven business days from the above date.

     If you cancel, any property traded, in any payments made by you under the contract or sale, and any negotiable instrument executed by you will be returned within 10 days following receipt by the seller of your cancellation notice, and any security interest arising out of the transaction will be canceled.

     If you cancel, you must make available to the seller at your residence, in substantially as good condition as when received, any goods delivered to you under this contract or sale, or you may, if you wish, comply with the instructions of the seller regarding the return shipment of the goods at the seller's expense and risk.

     If you do make the goods available to the seller and the seller does not pick them up them up within 20 days of the date of your notice of cancellation, you may retain or dispose of the goods without any further obligation. If you fail to make the goods available to the seller, or if you agree to return the goods to the seller and fail to do so, then you remain liable for performance of all obligations under the contract

     To cancel this transaction, mail or deliver a signed and dated copy of this cancellation notice, or any other written notice, or send a telegram to

_____
(Name of Seller)

at

_____
(Address of Sellers Place of Business)

not later than midnight of

_____
(Date)

I hereby cancel this transaction

_____ **/ / 2002** _____
(Date)

       X
_____
(Buyer's Signature)

I (we each) acknowledge receipt of two copies of this form.

Buyer: **X** _____   Buyer: **X** _____

I'll Do It Differently Next Time. . .

WAIVER OF RIGHT TO CANCEL

This form complies with professional standards in effect January 1-December 31, 2002

Having initiated a contract in connection with emergency repairs or service, for the immediate protection of persons or real and personal property with

_____
(Contractor)

for _____
(Owners Name)

at _____
(Address)

_____ , _____ , _____
(City)   (State)   (Zip)

I hereby state that the following emergency situation exists, requiring immediate attention, described as:

Pursuant to Section 1689.13 of the California Civil Code, I acknowledge and hereby waive all rights to cancel the sale within three days.

X_____   X_____
(Signature)   (Signature)

_____ 2002   _____ 2002
(Date)   (Date)

Chapter 15

Getting Ready for the Work to Begin

Properly preparing your home for the workmen, products, and materials before the work begins is strongly recommended. Hopefully the contractor you've hired has given you sufficient notice of when work will begin, so take the necessary steps to get your home ready.

For starters, take jewelry, cash, and anything else of value that is small and could be taken off the property and lock them up in a home safe. Although the contractor and his crew are perceived to be honest, don't tempt them with a watch or cash lying on the kitchen counter, or on a dresser.

Remove all weapons from the premises or lock them up. I know you want to trust everybody, but sometimes the fascination of a firearm may erupt into an unpleasant issue. Don't take the risk.

Move or cover electronic equipment and furniture from the areas where the workmen will be working. There will be dust from the work, so don't take the risk of dust damaging your property. If it is going to be a long project of four to eight weeks, remove the electronics and furniture to another area of the house. If it is not in the work area, it won't get damaged.

Prepare a bathroom for the workmen to use. They'll appreciate the toilet paper, towels, soap, and a designated place to wash up.

Decide where to put your pets during the time the work is going on. The workmen don't want to be responsible for your dogs or cats, and shouldn't have to be. They've got a job to do, and chasing your pets down the street is not one of them. Besides, you don't need a lawsuit if your pet bites or scratches someone. In addition, I'm sure your pets don't need the added stress and would appreciate your consideration.

Have your funds available as the job progresses. You want the contractor to be diligent and work through completion, and he wants to get paid as he reaches the agreed upon milestones. Don't aggravate the relationship by not holding up your end of the bargain.

Try to remember the names of the workman. They'll appreciate the respect you give them by calling them by their names. And don't forget to keep soft drinks or water and snacks around and available for the crews. You'll be surprised how much better they will work for you with a few refreshments coming their way. Your respect for them and their efforts will pay big dividends.

Keep your small valuables and firearms away from the workman

Getting Ready for the Work to Begin

Cover, or move, electronic equipment and furniture

Keep pets away from the work and the crews

Show the workmen respect for best results

Chapter 16

Monitoring the Progress

If a government agency has issued a permit for the home improvement work, they will inspect the work when it has reached a certain, specific stage. It will be the responsibility of whoever pulled the permit to call for the inspections. Hopefully, it will be the responsibility of the contractor you hired, not you.

These inspections are done to insure that completed work meets building codes. These inspections are not made to determine good quality work, only that the completed work meets code requirements. If possible, try to be present when inspections are made. If the workmanship passes inspection, you will be assured the work was done correctly. If you do not pass the inspection, you will be privy to what corrections need to be made and what type of work needs to be redone, and what type of time delays may occur. Don't be afraid to talk with the inspector and ask questions about a failed inspection. You'll gain some construction knowledge and it will help you understand the degree of the correction requirement. A minor correction requirement should not concern you, and your feelings toward your contractor, but a major correction requirement should raise a red flag about the competency of your contractor or your architect. When hiring a competent contractor or architect, there should not be any major surprises once the project begins.

The contractor is responsible for the quality of the workmanship, but so are you. You need to walk the project at the end of each day, with the workman responsible. You should verify accuracy of the project versus the approved plans, inspect the quality of the finished work for defects, and verify that all parts of the agreement are being fulfilled including keeping your property clean and safe. Professionally discuss areas of concern or deficiencies in quality with the crew leader as you see them. They'll usually agree with you and make the necessary improvements, repairs, or changes.

There are a few methods of monitoring the progress of the project that do not work very well. Standing behind, or next to, the workmen and giving them instruction or critiquing their work every four to five minutes is extremely nerve wracking for the worker. He'll never do his work as well as he would if you left him alone. Screaming and yelling, ranting and raving, seldom does anything besides cause the workers to want to get off your property as soon as possible. For best results, talk to and treat the workers the same way you'd like to be treated at your job.

Inspections by building officials will verify that work meets, or surpasses, code requirements, and have nothing to do with whether the work is of good quality or not

Both you and the contractor are responsible for the quality of the work being done

Let the contractors do their work. Do your walk-through and quality checks with the crew leader at the appropriate time

Chapter 17

Making Changes to the Project

Often there will be changes on the project as it progress. Sometimes you'll make a design change, sometimes the building officials or inspectors will require you to make a change, sometimes the contractor will request to make a change.

Regardless of the situation, any and all changes need to be in writing, stating exactly what the changes will be, the additional costs or reduced costs due to changes, and, if necessary, a drawing of the changes for your approval. Both you and the contractor must sign the change order, and you should each get a copy for your respective files. No exceptions.

In addition, the change order must specify the additional time required to complete the project. I've included examples of change order forms at the end of the chapter.

> Change orders must be in writing
>
> Both parties must sign change orders

I'll Do It Differently Next Time. . .

CONTRACT CHANGE ORDER
This form complies with professional standards in effect January 1-December 31, 2002

☐OWNER ☐ARCHITECT ☐CONTRACTOR ☐FIELD ☐OTHER

PROJECT:

_____
(Name)

_____
(Address)

_____
(City, State, Zip)

_____
(Phone)   (Fax)

CONTRACTOR:

_____
(Name)

_____
(Address)

_____
(City, State, Zip)

_____
(Phone)   (Fax)

The Contract is hereby modified and amended as follows:
It is mutually agreed that the contract price is: ☐ increased ☐ decreased by $ _____ ☐ payable ☐ deductible immediately upon completion of the work called for in this Change Order.

As a result of this Change Order, the time for completion of the above-mentioned contract is hereby extended by an additional _____ days.

This Change Order is incorporated into and governed by the above mentioned contract and is incorporated therein.

X _____   X _____
(Contractor/Owner)   Date   (Owner/Contractor)   Date

Making Changes to the Project

CHANGE ORDER   No. _____

This form complies with professional standards in effect January 1-December 31, 2002

Contractor: _____

License No: _____

OWNER'S NAME		PHONE	DATE /01	
STREET		JOB NAME		JOB NUMBER
CITY	STATE	STREET		
EXISTING CONTRACT NUMBER	DATE OF EXISTING CONTRACT	CITY		STATE

Add ___ calendar days to contract completion date.

ADDITIONAL CHARGE FOR ABOVE WORK IS: $ _____

Payment will be made as follows: _____
Above additional work to be performed under same conditions as specified in original contract unless otherwise stipulated.

Date _____ 2002 Authorizing Signature X_____
(OWNER SIGNS HERE)

We hereby agree to furnish labor and materials - complete in accordance with the above specifications, at above stated price.

Authorized Signature _____ Date   , 2002

NOTE: This Revision becomes part of, and in conformance with, the existing contract.

Chapter 18

Protecting Yourself and Your Property During the Work

One of the most common problems encountered during the work stage of a home improvement occurs when the homeowner gets sloppy with the money. As discussed earlier, the contractor should only get progress payments as he meets milestones. No exceptions.

The other financial area to be concerned with is preliminary liens, and mechanics' and materialmens' liens, that may occur during the process. The majority of states have laws regarding liens placed against property by customers or suppliers. These laws are an attempt to protect homeowners from financial hardship that may occur due to contractors that mismanage funds from projects or are unethical.

Basically, a lien is a claim filed against your property for payment which the subcontractor or material supplier maintains is owed by the property owner. If not paid, your property may be foreclosed by legal action and your property may be sold to pay the amount owed.

Even if you have paid your contractor in accordance with the terms of the contract, if the contractor fails to pay the subcontractors, material suppliers who performed work, or supplied materials in connection with your project, you still have the risk of a Mechanic's Lien being filed against your home and it possibly being foreclosed upon. This could result in you paying an invoice twice to satisfy the person or company that did not get paid by your contractor.

Shortly after your project begins, you will probably receive preliminary lien notices (see document at the end of this chapter) from subcontractors and material suppliers. Don't panic, this does not mean that a lien has been filed against your property. The law requires you be furnished with these notices to alert you that those individuals who have worked on your property, or have supplied materials for your project, may have lien rights. A preliminary lien by a subcontractor or material supplier must be filed with twenty days of the time their work is completed or materials were delivered.

It is an excellent practice to ask the contractor during the interviewing process if any subcontractors will be used, or if a material supplier will be delivering anything to your home. It will be important to know going into the project how your contractor conducts business and how you need to mange the process. If he is using subcontractors, or having materials delivered to your jobsite, specify in the contract that the contractor is responsible for obtaining lien releases from each of the subcontractors and material suppliers as work progresses, and as each phase of the project is completed and paid for. Then it will be your responsibility to collect the lien releases from the contractor you hired.

There are two types of lien releases. A Conditional Waiver and Release when signed off by a supplier, the company, or by those that performed labor, protects your property and relieves you of the obligation for payment of any claim filed for the period of time, or the amount of money, covered by the release. The release only becomes effective when the check, properly endorsed, has cleared the bank. In other words, the release is conditional upon the funds clearing the bank. The Conditional Waiver and Release can be used for both progress payments and final payments.

An Unconditional Waiver and Release also protects your property and relieves you of the obligation for payment of any claim filed for the period of time or the amount of money, covered by the release, but this document waives the rights of the supplier, the company, and those that performed labor, unconditionally and states that they have been paid for giving up those rights. You should not ask for, nor should the contractor use, an unconditional waiver and release until funds have cleared the bank. Similar to the Conditional Waiver and Release, the Unconditional Waiver and Release can be used for progress payments and final payments.

All Conditional and Unconditional Waiver and Release forms are shown at the end of this chapter.

I'll Do It Differently Next Time. . .

Another way to reduce the risk is by protecting yourself with a funding control company, but the risk will not be entirely eliminated unless you receive a conditional or unconditional waiver and release.

> Pay the contractor only as he reaches agreed upon milestones
>
> Ask for conditional waivers and releases upon payments to the suppliers, laborers, subcontractors, and the contractor
>
> Ask for Unconditional Waivers and Releases upon your check clearing the bank.

Protecting Yourself and Your Property During the Work

CALIFORNIA PRELIMINARY NOTICE

This form complies with professional standards in effect January 1-December 31, 2002
IN ACCORDANCE WITH SECTION 3097 AND 3098, CALIFORNIA CIVIL CODE
THIS IS NOT A LIEN, THIS IS NOT A REFLECTION ON THE INTEGRITY OF ANY CONTRACTOR OR SUBCONTRACTOR

YOU ARE HEREBY NOTIFIED THAT ...

_____
(name of person or firm furnishing labor, services, equipment or material)

CONSTRUCTION LENDER or
Reputed Construction Lender, if any

_____
(address of person or firm furnishing labor, services, equipment or material)

has furnished or will furnish labor, services, equipment or materials of the following general description:

_____
(general description of the labor, services, equipment or material furnished or to be furnished)

for the building, structure or other work of improvement located at:

_____
(address or description of job site sufficient for identification)

the name of the person or firm who contracted for the purchase of such labor, services, equipment or material is:

_____
(name and address of person or firm)

OWNER   or   **PUBLIC AGENCY**
or reputed owner   (on public work)
(on private work)

An estimate of the total price of the labor, services, equipment or materials furnished or to be furnished is:
$
(Dollar amount must be furnished to construction lender - optional as to owner or contractor)

Trust Funds to which Supplemental Fringe Benefits are payable.   (Material men not required to furnish)

_____ (name)   _____ (address)

CONSTRUCTION LOAN NO. _____ (if known)

_____ (name)   _____ (address)

_____ (name)   _____ (address)

ORIGINAL CONTRACTOR or
Reputed Contractor, if any

NOTICE TO PROPERTY OWNER
If bills are not paid in full for the labor, services, equipment, or materials furnished or to be furnished, a mechanic's lien leading to the loss, through court foreclosure proceedings, of all or part of your property being so improved may be placed against the property even though you have paid your contractor in full. You may wish to protect yourself against this consequence by (1) requiring your contractor to furnish a signed release by the person or firm giving you this notice before making payment to your contractor, or (2) any other method or device which is appropriate under the circumstances.

Dated: _____ /02

_____
Signature   (title)

Telephone Number

NOTE: COMPLETE DECLARATION OF SERVICE INFORMATION ON THE FOLLOWING PAGE OF THIS PART.

I'll Do It Differently Next Time. . .

CONDITIONAL WAIVER AND RELEASE UPON PROGRESS PAYMENT
[California Civil Code δ3262(d)(1)]
This form complies with professional standards in effect January 1-December 31, 2002

Upon receipt by the undersigned of a check from _____
(Your Customer)

in the sum of $ _____ payable to _____
(Amount of Check)   (Payee or Payees of Check)

and when the check has been properly endorsed and has been paid by the bank upon which it is drawn, this document shall become effective to release any Mechanic's Lien, Stop Notice, or Bond right the undersigned has on the job of _____
(Owner)

located at _____ to the following extent
(Job Description)

This release covers a progress payment for labor, services, equipment, and/or material furnished to
_____ through _____
(Your Customer)   (Date)

only and does not cover any retentions retained before or after the release date; extras furnished before the release date for which payment has not been received; extras or items furnished after the release date. Rights based upon work performed or items furnished under a written Change Order which has been fully executed by the parties prior to the release date are covered by this release unless specifically reserved by the claimant in this release. This release of any Mechanic's Lien, Stop Notice, or Bond right shall not otherwise affect the contract rights, including rights between parties to the contract based upon a rescission, abandonment, or breach of the contract, or the right of the undersigned to recover compensation for furnished labor, services, equipment, and/or material covered by this release if that furnished labor, services, equipment, and/or material was not compensated by the progress payment. Before any recipient of this document relies on it, said party should verify evidence of payment to the undersigned.

Dated: _____/02_____   _____
(Company Name)

X_____
(Signature)

_____
(Name/Title)

Note: *This form complies with the requirements of Civil Code Section 3252(d)(1). It is to be used by a party who applies for a progress payment when the progress payment check has not yet cleared the bank. This release only becomes effective when the check, properly endorsed, has cleared the bank.*

THE UNDERSIGNED HAVE PERFORMED LABOR FOR WAGES ON THE PROJECT DESCRIBED ABOVE AND HAVE BEEN PAID IN FULL TO DATE

(Signature Of Individual Performing Labor for Wages)	(Date)	(Signature Of Individual Performing Labor for Wages)	(Date)
(Signature Of Individual Performing Labor for Wages)	(Date)	(Signature Of Individual Performing Labor for Wages)	(Date)
(Signature Of Individual Performing Labor for Wages)	(Date)	(Signature Of Individual Performing Labor for Wages)	(Date)
(Signature Of Individual Performing Labor for Wages)	(Date)	(Signature Of Individual Performing Labor for Wages)	(Date)

Protecting Yourself and Your Property During the Work

CONDITIONAL WAIVER AND RELEASE UPON FINAL PAYMENT
[California Civil Code § 3262(d) (3)]
This form complies with professional standards in effect January 1-December 31, 2002

Upon receipt by the undersigned of a check from _____
(Your Customer)

in the sum of $ _____ payable to _____
(Amount of Check)   (Payee or Payees of Check)

and when the check has been properly endorsed and has been paid by the bank upon which it is drawn, this document shall become effective to release any Mechanic's Lien, Stop Notice, or Bond right the undersigned has for the job of _____
(Owner)

located at _____
(Job Description)

This release covers the final payment of the undersigned for all labor, services, equipment and/or material furnished on the job, except for disputed claims for additional work in the amount of $ _____

Before any recipient of this document relies on it, the party should verify evidence of payment to the undersigned.

Dated: _____ **/02**   _____
                                                        (Company Name)

_____   _____
(Signature)   (Name/Title)

NOTE: *This release is in accordance with the California Civil Code Section 3262 (d)(3). It is not effective until the check that constitutes final payment has been properly endorsed, and has cleared the bank.*

THE UNDERSIGNED HAVE PERFORMED LABOR FOR WAGES ON THE PROJECT DESCRIBED ABOVE AND HAVE BEEN PAID IN FULL TO DATE

(Signature Of Individual Performing Labor for Wages)	(Date)	(Signature Of Individual Performing Labor for Wages)	(Date)
(Signature Of Individual Performing Labor for Wages)	(Date)	(Signature Of Individual Performing Labor for Wages)	(Date)
(Signature Of Individual Performing Labor for Wages)	(Date)	(Signature Of Individual Performing Labor for Wages)	(Date)
(Signature Of Individual Performing Labor for Wages)	(Date)	(Signature Of Individual Performing Labor for Wages)	(Date)

NOTES:

I'll Do It Differently Next Time. . .

UNCONDITIONAL WAIVER AND RELEASE UPON PROGRESS PAYMENT
[California Civil Code § 3262(d)(2)]
This form complies with professional standards in effect January 1-December 31, 2002

The undersigned has been paid and has received a progress payment in the sum of $ _____

for labor, service, equipment, or material furnished to   _____
(Your Customer)

on the job of _____ located at _____
(Owner)   (Job Description)

and does hereby release any Mechanic's Lien, Stop Notice, or Bond right that the undersigned has on the above

referenced job to the following extent: This release covers a progress payment for labor, services, equipment, and/or

material furnished to _____ through _____ only and does not cover any
(Your Customer)   (Date)
retentions retained before or after the release date; extras furnished before the release date. Rights based upon work performed or items furnished under a written change order which has been fully executed by the parties prior to the release date are covered by this release unless specifically reserved by the claimant in this release. This release of any Mechanic's Lien, Stop Notice, or Bond right shall not otherwise affect the contract rights, including rights between parties to the contract based upon a rescission, abandonment, or breach of the contract, or the right of the undersigned to recover compensation for furnished labor, services, equipment, and/or material covered by this release if that furnished labor, services, equipment, and/or material covered by this release was not compensated by the progress payment.

Dated: _____ /02   _____
(Company Name)

                                     _____
(Signature)

                                     _____
(Name/Title)

NOTE: This form of release complies with the requirements of Civil Code Section 3262(d)(2). It is to be used to release claims to the extent that a progress payment has actually been received by the releasing party.

NOTICE: THIS DOCUMENT WAIVES RIGHTS UNCONDITIONALLY AND STATES THAT YOU HAVE BEEN PAID FOR GIVING UP THOSE RIGHTS. THIS DOCUMENT IS ENFORCEABLE AGAINST YOU IF YOU SIGN IT, EVEN IF YOU HAVE NOT BEEN PAID. IF YOU HAVE NOT BEEN PAID, USE A CONDITIONAL RELEASE FORM.

THE UNDERSIGNED HAVE PERFORMED LABOR FOR WAGES ON THE PROJECT DESCRIBED ABOVE AND HAVE BEEN PAID IN FULL TO DATE

(Signature Of Individual Performing Labor for Wages)	(Date)	(Signature Of Individual Performing Labor for Wages)	(Date)
(Signature Of Individual Performing Labor for Wages)	(Date)	(Signature Of Individual Performing Labor for Wages)	(Date)
(Signature Of Individual Performing Labor for Wages)	(Date)	(Signature Of Individual Performing Labor for Wages)	(Date)
(Signature Of Individual Performing Labor for Wages)	(Date)	(Signature Of Individual Performing Labor for Wages)	(Date)

NOTES:

Protecting Yourself and Your Property During the Work

UNCONDITIONAL WAIVER AND RELEASE UPON FINAL PAYMENT
[California Civil Code § 3262 (d)(4)]
This form complies with professional standards in effect January 1-December 31, 2002

The undersigned has been paid in full for all labor, services, equipment and/or material furnished to
_____ on the job of _____
             (Your Customer)   (Owner)

located at _____ and does hereby waive
                               (Job Description)

and release any right to a mechanic's lien, stop notice, or any right against a labor and/or material bond on the
job, except for disputed claims for extra work in the amount of $ _____

Dated: _____ **/02**   _____
                                               (Company Name)

_____   _____
             (Signature)   (Name/Title)

NOTE: This form of release complies with the requirements of Civil Code Section 3262(d)(4). It is to be used to release claims to the extent that a progress payment has actually been received by the releasing party.

NOTICE: THIS DOCUMENT WAIVES RIGHTS UNCONDITIONALLY AND STATES THAT YOU HAVE BEEN PAID FOR GIVING UP THOSE RIGHTS. THIS DOCUMENT IS ENFORCEABLE AGAINST YOU IF YOU SIGN IT, EVEN IF YOU HAVE NOT BEEN PAID. IF YOU HAVE NOT BEEN PAID, USE A CONDITIONAL RELEASE FORM.

THE UNDERSIGNED HAVE PERFORMED LABOR FOR WAGES ON THE PROJECT DESCRIBED ABOVE AND HAVE BEEN PAID IN FULL TO DATE

_____ _____   . _____ _____
(Signature Of Individual Performing Labor for Wages) (Date)   (Signature Of Individual Performing Labor for Wages) (Date)

_____ _____   _____ _____
(Signature Of Individual Performing Labor for Wages) (Date)   (Signature Of Individual Performing Labor for Wages) (Date)

_____ _____   _____ _____
(Signature Of Individual Performing Labor for Wages) (Date)   (Signature Of Individual Performing Labor for Wages) (Date)

_____ _____   _____ _____
(Signature Of Individual Performing Labor for Wages) (Date)   (Signature Of Individual Performing Labor for Wages) (Date)

NOTES:

Chapter 19

Record Keeping

Keep a job file of all papers relating to your project. It should include:

1. The contract
2. All plans, specifications, and drawings
3. All change orders
4. All bills and invoices
5. All cancelled checks
6. All waiver and releases from subcontractors, laborers, the contractor, and material suppliers'
7. All letters, forms, and correspondence with your contractor
8. A list of phone numbers for all subcontractors and material suppliers that were involved on your project

You should also keep records of each subcontractor who works on your project, what part of the work he performed, and how long he was on your project.

If a material supplier makes a delivery, write down the name of the company, the date of the delivery, and a general description of what was delivered. When you receive lien releases from the subcontractors or material suppliers, check them off against your list. This way you'll have a record of what was paid and what was not.

> Keep a file of all paper records from the project. You may need them at later date if a dispute arises

Chapter 20

The Completion of the Remodel

So, the work is complete, you're satisfied with the quality, and everybody has been paid.

Not so fast. There is one more step to complete the process.

A Notice of Completion needs to be recorded in the office of the county recorder, in the county in which the job site is located, within ten days after completion. (See Notice of Completion form at the end of this chapter) This step is probably the least used step in remodeling, but, none-the-less, it needs to be done to complete the process. The purpose of the Notice of Completion is to curtail the time allowed for a Mechanic's Lien to be placed on your property.

If the Notice of Completion is timely recorded, then the time within which a Mechanic's Lien may be recorded against the property is sixty days by prime contractors, and thirty days by subcontractors. If this notice is not recorded in a timely manner, prime contractors and sub-contractors have a ninety day period from the completion of the work in which to record their Mechanic's Lien.

I'll Do It Differently Next Time. . .

If there is more than one owner, the Notice of Completion must be signed by each co-owner. Any Notice of Completion signed by a successor in interest shall recite the names and addresses of his transferor or transferors.

You have now been educated and should understand the rules of remodeling. If you follow the rules outlined in this book, you'll eliminate the risks involved with remodeling your property. If you try and short cut the required steps involved or try to speed up the process though desperation or frustration, you'll surely add risk to your remodel. That risk could be very expensive.

I hope the information provided to you in my book is helpful. Good luck on your next project.

> File the Notice of Completion with the county recorder
>
> Congratulations

The Completion of the Remodel

NOTICE OF COMPLETION

(Notice pursuant to Civil Code Section 3093, must be recorded within 10 days after completion)
This form complies with professional standards in effect January 1-December 31, 2002

Notice is Hereby Given That:

1. The undersigned is an owner or agent of an owner of the interest or estate stated below.
2. The full name of the owner is
3. The full address of the owner is

4. The nature of the interest or estate of the owner is; in fee.

(If other than fee, strike "in fee" and insert, for example, "Purchaser Under Contract of Purchase," or Lease")
5. The full names and full addresses of all co-owners, if any, who hold any title or interest with the above-named owner in the property are:

NAMES   ADDRESSES

6. A work of improvement on the property hereinafter described was completed on

(Date)

The work done was:
7. The name of the contractor, if any, for such work of improvement is

(If no Contractor for work of improvement, insert "none")   (Date of Contract)
8. The street address of said property is

(If no street address has been assigned, insert "none")

County of _____, State of California, and is described as follows:

9. The property on which said work of improvement was completed is in the city of

DATE: _____ /02 _____   X _____
(Verification for individual owner)   (Signature of owner of agent of owner named in Paragraph 2)

VERIFICATION

I, undersigned, say: I am the

("President," "Owner," "Partner," "Manager," etc.)

the declarant of the foregoing Notice of Completion; I have read said Notice of Completion and know the contents thereof; the same

is true of my own knowledge.

I declare under penalty of perjury that the foregoing is true and correct.

Executed on _____, 2002, at _____, California.
(Date of Signature)   (City where Signed)

_____
(Personal signature of the individual who is swearing that the contents of the notice of completion are true)